LINES FROM COLLINGS HILL

Borgo Press Books by NELLIE HUNT COLLINGS

Lines from Collings Hill

LINES FROM COLLINGS HILL

POEMS, JOURNAL ENTRIES, AND SELECTED LIFE RECORDS

NELLIE HUNT COLLINGS

Edited and Arranged by Michael R. Collings

THE BORGO PRESS
MMXII

Borgo Laureate Series
ISSN 1082-3336
Number Ten

LINES FROM COLLINGS HILL

Copyright © 2001, 2012 by Michael R. Collings

FIRST BORGO PRESS EDITION

Published by Wildside Press LLC

www.wildsidebooks.com

DEDICATION

To the Collings Cousins,
no matter how many times removed

CONTENTS

INTRODUCTION 9
TO NELLIE—FROM THE PERSPECTIVE OF
    A CENTURY 13
ON FIRST SEEING PHOTOGRAPHS OF MY
    GRANDFATHER IN HIS MIDDLE-AGE . . . 15
LINES FROM COLLINGS HILL 17
APPENDIX I 131
APPENDIX II 139
APPENDIX III 143
INDEX OF NAMES AND POEMS 145

INTRODUCTION

The following pages contain all that I have been able to locate of the many verses written by my paternal grandmother, Nellie Hunt Collings. Most are drawn from one of two sources: 1) a typescript prepared by her youngest surviving son, Ralph Willard Collings (my father), sometime after her death, drawing on her handwritten journals, scrapbook, and other primary materials; and 2) a second typescript of just the poetry, prepared by Ralph Willard even later and mimeographed for a number of her descendants—the copies of this mimeographed version that I have seen are now almost illegible. Unfortunately, as far as I have been able to determine, most of the original materials were subsequently destroyed or have been lost.

Several months ago, another of Nellie's grandchildren, Brian Cooper, contacted me about a transcription he had made of the poems for an internet site—as a result of our email discussion, he sent me a copy of his transcription, which I added to the two already available to me. From these varied sources, then, comes this book, composed variously of Grandma Collings' poetry, segments of her journals that introduce, discuss, or otherwise relate to her poetry, photographs illustrating her life and her history, especially as they relate to the subjects of her poetry, and several life records—including the marriage certificate that, startling to many of her descendents, gives her full name as Nellie *Eliza* Hunt.

In part this project has been aimed at the dozens of cousins—first, second, and third, by now—who knew Nellie only as an elderly and increasingly frail woman...or who never knew her at all. By reproducing her verses and bits from her journal, I hope to help us all recover who she truly was, the kind of mind and spirit she preserved throughout her life, the compassion she felt for others' losses, and the joy she felt in their happiness.

In a larger part, however, *Lines from Collings Hill* is a personal tribute as well. I did not know until after her death that my grandmother wrote poetry. No one ever mentioned it; no one ever showed me one of her pieces; I have no recollection of *her* mentioning it. Of course, at thirteen, I was probably too young when she passed away to care much for poetry, but that perception has changed radically over the years. For over three decades now, I too have turned to poetry in times of sorrow and loss, of joy, of loneliness, of fear. And in doing so, I have discovered connections with my grandmother that I never imagined existed, I have felt nearer to her than ever before, and I have understood in greater detail the strengths that supported her throughout her life.

—Michael Robert Collings
Thousand Oaks CA
September 2001

TO NELLIE—FROM THE PERSPECTIVE OF A CENTURY

How lonely. How distressing.
A farmstead cabin trapped in snow,
No faces to see
But family—
No other voices, thoughts, minds
To share her dreams,
Her words.

How lonely. How distressing.
Day upon day no mail nesting in the
Rural box
Beyond
The gate where peeled cottonwood
Uprights took root
And grew.

How lonely. How distressing.
A daughter lost just as they began
To mesh in mind—
A son required

By war to travel over seas and then
Returned to wed
A distant love.

How lonely. How distressing.
To watch her one love age and twist—
To know her home
Once more as loss—
To feel a mind grow wretched and
Infirm—then vague—
And finally gone

How lonely. How distressing.
To know her only through old blurring
Photographs—see
Her but not hear her,
Not partake of laughter, wit,
Or voice, or heart,
Or Poetry.

> —Michael R. Collings,
> With Love

ON FIRST SEEING PHOTOGRAPHS OF MY GRANDFATHER IN HIS MIDDLE-AGE

He always seems unfinished—cheeks
Rough with whitened whiskers, hair
Corn-shock coarse and peppered black
On white, lips thin and quavering and
Querulous in coming age. Even when
I see him young, ambitious, smooth,
Eager to consume the world;
Or later, hearth-black by his forge,
Leather apron glossy in the heat;
Or later still a hatted silhouette
Among the corn—even then
There is about him that which cries
For grinder, sander, lathe, and polish to
Finish incompleteness—give him life.

—Michael R. Collings
With Love

LINES FROM
COLLINGS HILL

I, **Nellie Elida Hunt**, was born in Monroe, Utah 4 Mar. 1883, the third child of Emily Casto and Moroni Hunt. At the time of my birth my mother was nearly 20, lacking 19 days, my father was nearly 31.[1]

* * * * * * *

Maggie Warnock was my first teacher. We went to school in a small rock building, I think it is known as the "Town Hall." It is just south of the present school House. There was an old wooden black board, charts, maps, and a water bucket and dipper in one corner of the room. The seats were made of rough lumber, made to hold two children, but my two brothers and I sat in

---

1. Nellie was born Nellie Eliza Hunt, according to the Monroe Ward Membership Records and the Marriage License signed in their hands by both Mother and Dad. She didn't like the name so changed it some time during her adolescence—RWC

one seat. We marched up to the front of the room, and read our lessons from a chart all in concert:

> Good bye, little rake, Good bye little hoe
> Up in the attic you must go.

* * * * * * *

I haven't mentioned that the Spanish American War took place in 1898. I shall never forget when my brother Alvin woke us up in the night to tell us about the destruction of the "Maine". You can read about that in your history. I was about 15 then....

Going back to the war again, the night they had a farewell party for the boys, I wanted to go to the dance, but my parents wouldn't let me. Ed and Alvie went. After they left I wrote the first verse I had ever written, called "The Boys in Blue". The next morning I read them to Ma, and she had me read them to Pa, I can see him now, with the tears standing in his eyes. Next I wrote a poem called "Remember the Maine," I wrote one about Amy, only I used the name of Milly in it. I finally got me a notebook to write my poems in, but one winter in school some one "swiped" it or it was lost, I don't remember which.

Ed, George, Alvin, Howard, and Nellie Hunt, about 1887

Spring 1900

About this time in my life I wrote a poem called "Two Flowers". I sent it to Salt Lake City to the Deseret Sunday School Union Board. I was afraid they wouldn't publish it and I didn't want anyone to make fun of it, so I never told any one, not even Mother or Janie. It was printed all right, but I [didn't] find out about it until years after. Here it is:

Two Flowers

By the old stone wall in the garden two flowers grew
    side by side
One was a beautiful rosebud, whose beauty, alas, was
    her pride.
The other, a fair sweet lily of such a modest hue,
Who lived for the love she gave and received and the
    good that she could do.

The rose bud was discontented with the simple life she
    led,
Warmed by the gentle sunbeam and by the dew drops
    fed.
She never thought of thanking the sun for his gentle
    ray
And gave no heed to the Zephyr who kindly came her
    way.

Tired of peaceful solitude, she longed to go away
Far from her safe and quiet homes and live a life so

gay.
One day a stranger passing, from her stem the sweet rose tore,
And that haughty flower's thankless heart was quickly stationed o'er

[Proudly content in her new career, unreasoning helpless thing,
Felt she no shame at that rude caress, no keen resentful sting
She knew she was leaving her birthplace, the lonely little spot,
But her heart had gained its fond wish, for which it long had sought.][2]

Into the brilliant ballroom he carried the blossom fair,
Then farther into the gay saloon, with its vile and stifling air,
But her beautiful color faded, her breath no longer sweet,
And the careless hand that had plucked her, cast her out in the stony street.

Alone in the cold dark gutter, unwept and unhonored she died
This beautiful rosebud, whose beauty, alas, was her pride.

---

2. This stanza is included in RWC's transcription of the poems, but not in his transcription of the journals themselves.

"Just a pretty flower, Mama," was the dying baby's call.
And the mother found the lily by the Old Stone Wall.
The flower was placed in the Darling's hand and together they died the two,
The lily grateful and full of joy for the good that she could do.

[Aged 17, 1900, written in Monroe, Utah]

Nov. 4, 1904

My Dear Nellie:—I received your most welcome letter this morning as the train was late last night I did not go to the office until this morning and I can tell you I was glad to hear from you again, to know that you are well and getting along as well as you are. I am well and getting along nicely, as I have changed boarding places, and am staying with my sister Alice at present, but working for father just the same.... I wish you were here this evening for there is a grand theater on and I guess every body is having a gay time. By the way where in the world did you find that sweet little piece of poetry....

Happiness—A Recipe

To make it: Take a hall dimly lit;
A pair of stairs where two can sit;
Or soft music, a bar or so;
Two spoons of—to spoons you know
Of little love pats, one or two,
Or one squeezed hand, instead, will do;
A waist—the size to be embraced!
Two ripe lips rose red, to taste;
And if the lips are soft and sweet
You'll find your happiness complete.

—Selected

Ralph Collings, about 1903

1910

Since I was a girl in school I have been putting together some verses, even submitting some to the church magazines but only receiving the usual rejection slips. However, one was printed, unknown to me for many years as I have already written, but I have continued to put words to rhyme ever since and have given them or read them at specific occasions. A few years ago when Zelda Newby lost her little baby I wrote these lines and gave them to her. Since then I have used these words of consolation to help other sorrowing mothers. Today I wrote it out for Gwendolyn La Rocke—May 6, 1940.

Sunbeam

Like a ray of sunshine, sent from the realms above,
Came your sweet little baby breathing a message of love.
Like a sunbeam earthward bound she came to cheer your souls
And a place in your hearts found.

She has gone to Heaven again you cannot see her now;
But still a ray of Heavenly light is lingering on your brow.
Your beautiful little Darling came not here to stay,
But like the golden sunbeams, to drive your cares away.

Though the darkness is about you, cry not in wild
 dismay
For the One who stilled the billows, will roll the clouds
 away;
All about is dark and dreary, but Dear Friends, hope
 on! hope on!
Remember the night is darkest, just before the Dawn.

As the Shepherd carries the little lamb over the desert
 wide,
The mother will ever be found hovering eagerly at His
 side
Up where the grass is green and sweet with the morning
 dew,
Your little lamb has gone and is waiting there for you.

>   (This poem was written in the year 1910 for Zelda Brown [Newby] when her baby died. I have copied it for a few others.)

May 1910

A Missionary Poem

God has called you forth, Dear Brother,
His grand message to proclaim
In the Name of Christ, Our Saviour,
In his Own Dear Holy Name

Go you forth, then O! Dear Brother
With a heart that's brave and true
Go you Forth and do your duty
Do the work God bids you do.

Like a brave and valiant soldier
Brother Dearest, may you stand
Ready at a moments notice
To obey His great command

God Bless you then, Dear Brother,
And protect you on your way
That you may return in safety
Brother, we shall ever pray.

If for learning you are seeking
That, Dear Brother, you will find
For to know the ways of God
Would be knowledge most divine.

Whether on a distant shore,
Or out on the ocean foam,

Remember still, Dear Brother,
That we'll think of you at home.

    (Monroe, Utah—written for my brother George M[atthew] Hunt—May 2, 1910 when he was leaving to go on his mission to Germany.)

March 1913

...Ralph returned to work, but I think he had been laid off at Garfield and had gone on to Johnson to find work, but had not been very successful for I wrote this letter to him

Monroe, Utah
Mar. 1, 1913

Mr. Ralph Collings
Johnson, Utah

My dear sweetheart:—I was indeed sorry to hear that you had to meet with another disappointment so soon. I couldn't sleep at all for thinking about the first night I heard it. They say life is a dear school and by the way things go you ought to get something out of it. Well, to my notion, mistakes, failures, and bad luck are a great deal better than nothing! They at least show a willing heart and hand and when we show our God that we are working for some purpose if it is ever so humble he will indeed help us. You are no doubt anxious to hear how we are getting along at home, we so far have had no luck at all....

....With great big love and lots of love and kisses from your Darling Nellie and babies.

       Amy's x x x x x x x
       Dallin's x x x x x x
       Wardies x x x x x x
       Little Nell's x x x x

I got to thinking about all Ralph's disappointments so I started composing a poem and finally came up with the following:

To My Dear Husband

When you go to your work in the morn, go with a brave cheerful heart,
Remember that half of the battle depends on the way you start.

At night when your work is over, and you sit and think o'er it all;
Let no shadow of sorrow or regret on your bright pathway fall.

But each fair day that you're toiling for dear little babies and me,
Just think how I long to be doing something, "My Sweetheart" for thee.

We can't do much toward helping; in fact, there's only one way,
And that is to love you forever, 'Say Papa', How's that for pay.

Monroe, Utah—1913[3]

---

3. RWC's transcription gives 1914, but Nellie's journals place the poem directly after her letter of 1 March 1913 to Ralph at Johnson, Utah.

Nellie and Ralph Collings shortly after their wedding, 1906

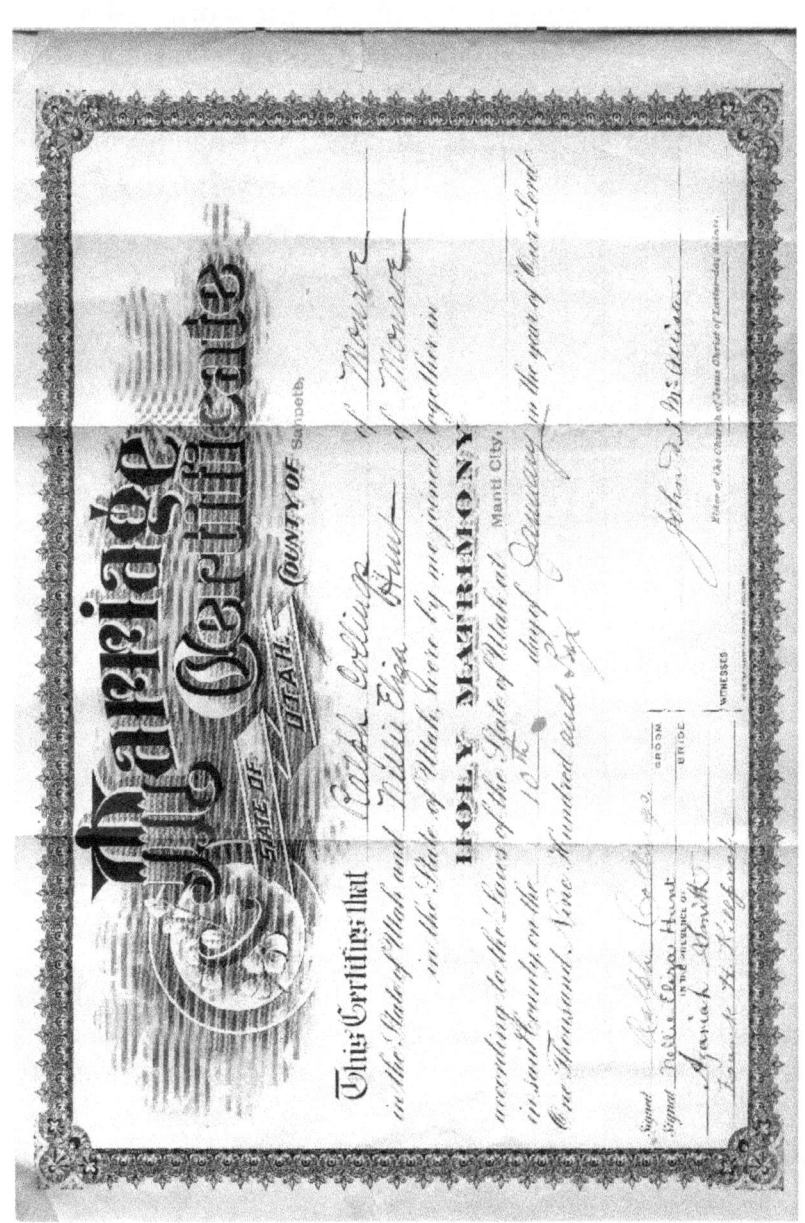

Computer scan of Ralph and Nellie's original marriage Certificate, 10 January 1906.

Note her signature in the lower left-hand corner, clearly reading *Nellie Eliza Hunt.*

About 1910

Mountain Rose

As I walked through the fields, I beheld a beautiful blossom fair.
It was a bud just unfolding, its petals bright and rare.
I thought as I gazed on this flower as it grew in this garden of ours
It was a type, a wonderful type, of God's most beautiful flowers.

There in our little garden, this little rose bud grew,
Warmed by the summer sunshine, cooled by the morning dew,
Fairest flower that grows, we loved it—
We cared for this blossom, we called it Our Sweet Mountain Rose.

But the Master came to our fields one day and beheld our blossom rare
A beautiful Godlike treasure so He took it within his care.
Our hearts are sad—but our hearts have been sad before;
When another fair sweet flower bloomed on that bright happy shore.

Just beyond the eternal walls there is the richer ground,
Blooming in his garden may the fairest flowers be found

Side by side, by the gateway growing in sweet repose,
Stands a graceful, snow-white lily and a beautiful mountain Rose.

> (Monroe, Utah—Written for Ed Naser and family when his little Rose died. His little Lily Grace died when I was about 10 years old.)

About 1910

...I was still lamenting the loss of our little Nelda [2 January 1913] and considered a little poem that I had written four years before for Thomas Ransom's in commemoration of their little [one] as most appropriate for ourselves at this time:

Our Little Bird

One of our birds has gone away; it has flown away from our breast.
One little bird has gone from us; it has flown from the dear home nest.
It's not lost, this beautiful bird, this beautiful bird of ours,
Tis gone to the land of the bright sunshine, gone to the land of flowers.

Down in our nest we sheltered it, safely under our wing;
Tenderly there we guarded it, then we bid our sweet birdie sing;
But the blasts of winter blew cold, and dark was the dismal rain,
Tho we held her close 'neath our breast, our loved one quivered with pain.

When we saw that she was suffering, then we bid our sweet bird go;
We weep, not because she is lost to us, but because we

love her so.
She has gone to the realm of the warm sunshine, gone to the land of rest;
There 'mid the beautiful flowers, she will build for us all a dear nest.

When the time comes for departing, swiftly we'll take our wing
And we'll wend our way to the beautiful land, where the birds forever sing,
When we have left our nest, our little nest here below,
We will all enter into the Heavenly Realm of the One who loves us so.

> (Monroe, Utah—Written in remembrance of Thos. Ransom's little girl. She died in about 1912)

1916

In 1916 when Delile Jones, Vern Jones' little daughter died in Idaho, I sent them these words of condolence:

A Token of Love—"For Nonie"

Your heads are bowed down in sorrow,
Your hearts are now filled with pain
For one whom you loved, O! so dearly,
In her grave you have peacefully lain.

At the gates of the poor and the lowly,
At the portals of the rich and the gay
When death and sorrow enters
There is none can answer them "Nay!"

There's no fleeing away from our troubles,
No hiding away from our care;
But the wise and the strong, are those
Who bravely life's trials bear.

May the tears you are shedding
Bring to your hearts sweet repose
As the dew fresh from Heaven
Revives and brightens the rose.

Would it comfort you, Brother and Sister,
Would it sooth your pain if you knew
That our hearts and sympathies
Are both, dearest Friends, with you?

April 1921

A Prayer

Out of my heart, I'll utter a prayer,
For all that is good and grand,
For those who are meek, and souls that seek
The clasp of a brother's hand.

I pray for souls that are glad or sad
Or for souls that long to be free.
O! World so great: O! World so strong
May I offer a prayer for thee.

O! Words that I say, Will you bring I pray
To some sad heart sweet bliss?
Fall soft I pray, as a summer day
Or a Mother's tender kiss.

Tho, sorrow and strife, may cloud my life
Come true, my dreams never may;
But for hearts that ache, and hearts that break,
Teach me, O! Lord to Pray.

>(Written in Monroe, Utah and read at G. C.'s funeral in Venice, Utah, April 1, 1921)

1923-1925

While in Centerfield I wrote a number of poems. I have them in my scrap book. They used to call on me to give readings in Relief Society meetings. They were having a party for some of the members who had taken part in a little play called, "Our Neighbor," so I wrote some verses about the different ones in the play, after that I had a fairly steady job of it.

* * * * * * *

In 1925 I also composed some verses in memory of my little black-haired baby, Burton Hunt Collings:

That Dear Little Boy of Mine[4]

I am sitting tonight in the twilight, he sun has sunk in the west,
And the mother bird has flown again safely back to her own home nest.
O'er me steals a feeling—a feeling, all divine,
My heart doth yearn, as my thoughts return
To that Dear Little Boy of mine.

Tonight my heart is full of peace; it is often filled with pain,
When I think of my boy, My Dear Little Boy who will

---

4. Both typescript versions of this poem present editorial difficulties, especially in meter and rhyme. Because of the repetition of the title as the final line of each stanza, I have chosen a five-line format with internal and end rhyme in the fourth line. MRC

never come back again.
Dear Lord, My soul, My heart is Thine,
Help me each day to seek the way,
To that Dear Little Boy of Mine.

Sorrow oft times helps us to feel another's woe. My own wee Laddie had scarce gone to rest
Till another mother's baby lay dying on my breast.
I told her of the Master; of His Love Divine,
And I shed a tear, as my thoughts drew near
To that Dear Little boy of Mine.

As I soothed this weeping Mother, methought my heart would break,
As I told her of the Saviour, who suffered for her sake;
And how He loved His children of every clime,
Tho' my soul was tired, the thoughts were inspired,
By that Dear Little Boy of Mine.

>(Written about Burton Hunt Collings, born April 8, 1919 in Monroe, Utah and died May 16, 1921 in Monroe Utah—written in 1925 in Centerfield, Utah)

Burton Hunt Collings, early in 1921

Before we had left Our Little Home in south Monroe, our Mexican neighbor, Bro. Chavez, living on the south side of our lot, died, leaving several small children, so I wrote this poem in hopes of consoling the bereaved and dispairing family:

A Token of Love

Within the Master's garden I am resting for a while,
With his gentle arms about me I can see his gracious smile.
I have passed beyond the gateway of the weary road of strife,
And at peace I now am resting from the weary cares of life.

Do not think that I have left you to struggle all alone,
For among God's many mansions I'll select for you a home.
Within this lovely Kingdom where the roses bloom so fair
I have only come before you, a bright home to prepare.

Be kind to your mother, I would ask, O! Children dear,
Smooth from her brow all sorrow, wipe from her eye the tear.
Farewell, Wife and Children, now I bid you all adieu,
When God calls you to his kingdom, I'll be waiting there for you.

(Monroe, Utah—1919)

Hearts Bereft

I weep for you, dear, dear friends,
To you my sympathy I send.
Of trouble, you have had your share,
But this is more than you can bear.

'Tis hard to have our loved ones go,
Yet who can tell another's woe;
Just give to God your heart, your hand,
For He alone will understand.

Weep, let thy tears fall like rain
For tears will oft times soothe the pain;
Be brave, dear friends, be brave and true;
God has a mission here for you.

Perhaps dear hearts, in after years,
God Himself will dry your tears;
My words, alas, are all in vain,
Nothing but time can ease your pain.

O! I would ask that Heaven send
Comfort to you—unhappy friends,
May His great Light upon you shine
And fill your soul with peace divine.

(Centerfield, Utah—1924)

Little Virginia

God, in His mercy, has now on thee smiled,
Little Virginia, so sweet and so mild.
Sweet was the mission God had thee to do,
Darling, too soon, thy dear mission was thru.[5]

Thy little hands 'round our heart strings twine,
Thy little eyes from the Heavens shine.
Angels have called thee to Missions[6] above,
Little Virginia, sweet flower of love.

Like a wee bird, from thy nest, thou hast flown,
Leaving thy parents and loved ones alone.

When Life's work is o'er, and Life's battles thru,
Little Virginia, we're coming for you.

May we be, Father, meek and mild,
Guided to Heaven by this little child
Where thou art now, we wish to go,
Little Virginia, spotless as snow.

When we, at last, to God's Portals come,
Little Virginia, welcome us home.

---

5. At this point, RWC's original typescript deletes the lines:
Thou art an angel, who once was a child,
Little Virginia, so sweet and so mild.

6. Alternate reading: 'Mansions above."

I wrote the above lines for one of my dearest friends, Lora Tuft, who had lost her little granddaughter. (I have copied it out for several other babies since them. Last written on May 5, 1940. I copied it again for Bishop A. Leo Olson's baby in Jerome, Idaho in 1949, and again for Joyce Pettit's baby on August 21, 1957.

About 1925/26

Just about the time I was getting to I could take a little pleasure and comfort in my Amy, she got married. Some time before her marriage, I had felt that I was losing contact with each other and had written these lines:

My Lost Love

'Twas in the sweet, sweet long ago, there lived a child that I loved so,
And Ah, it seemed as if to me this fair sweet child, then loved me.
I taught her to be good and true, of life, I taught her all I knew,
If some small favor I denied, and she perchance in sorrow cried
And tho it caused her bitter pain she seemed to love me just the same.
For fourteen years, perhaps, or more she played beside my cottage door.
And often we strolled hand in hand, each other's sorrows to understand;
But peace and joy cannot ever last, a shadow o'er our path was cast.

Just when it came I never knew, so faint at first it grew, and grew;
And then one day to my surprise, a stranger gazed into my eyes.

She had my daughter's form and face, but a stranger sat there in her place.
Yet though she sat beside my knee! she seemed a thousand miles from me.
Gone were the happy days of bliss, when pain was cured with a kiss,
I tried, I tried, alas, in vain, I couldn't reach her heart again.
Though 'twas my fault I know, this did not seem to soothe my woe.
I tried to do the best I could—my efforts were misunderstood.

O! There is naught in Heaven above, as patient as a Mother's Love,
I seem to know, I seem to feel, that some day, at my feet she'll kneel;
She then will whisper soft and low, "I love you," as in long ago.
Perhaps when she is older grown, and her love for pleasures, then has flown.
Her love will then come back to me, e'en tho she's far across the sea;
Perhaps it'll be in after years, when death has brushed away my tears;
And tho I've passed beyond the tide, the gulf twixt life and death is wide,
'Tis then that she will take my hand and whisper, "Dear, I understand."
Her love will then come back to me e'en through the veil of mystery—

You ask me, why I seem to know, I think perhaps—
God told me so!

(Centerfield, Utah, 1925-26)

Amy Collings, about 1920

About March 1926

Our Annual Day

Glorious day, Our Annual Day, a Sacred Day, thou art,
By God's most holy Prophet was this day set apart.
A few of God's handmaidens met there in fair Nauvoo
To found an organization in Eighteen Forty Two.

Tho they were weak and timid, they had no need to fear,
For within that Holy assemblage they knew that God was near.
They were few in number, yet they bowed in humble prayer,
Where few are gathered in His name, Our Father will be there.

Relief Society, Thy name we now revere,
A calling from on High to give comfort; aid and cheer.
And we have met today to celebrate the birth
Of as grand an organization as ever graced the earth.

O! Sisterhood, O! Sisterhood, Our songs of praise we give
To this great noble work, O! May it ever live!

> (Written and read on the 17th of March about 1926 in Centerfield, Utah)

The Home Dramatic Company

It was on the Seventeenth of March, it was on our Annual Day,
That the Home Dramatic Company staged a most successful play.

"My Neighbors," was the title of that dear little comedy,
And the way they put it over was wonderful to see.
Of their work and efforts we all feel very proud
And so we'll sing their praises and we'll sing them good and loud!

When it comes to comic acting, just call on Sister Jean,
Why, in the part of "Peter," she was just a scream.
She'd be a great comedian if she had half a chance,
She'd be a Charlie Chaplin if she had his shoes and pants.

And Edna Bardsley, too, comes in for her share,
With her braids and cunning ribbons and her blue-eyed baby stare.
Now don't forget Talitha, that shy, roguish elf.
She acted so darn natural that she acted like her self.

Ester Jergensen, as "Ezra," sure made us grin,
Why, she took her part so manly with the whiskers on her chin.
Sister Anderson, as Grandma, was simply sublime,

With her rug-rags, and match-making, she made me think of mine.

Now please don't misunderstand this silly little rhyme,
Of course, I meant my Grandma, not any love affairs of mine.
Eva Jenson, as "Mrs. Averill," created lots of fun.
I've been wondering ever since, Did she get her ironing done?

Sister Bemis, as one of "The Neighbors," comes in for her share of fame.
She was the lame old lady, tho her acting wasn't lame.

Sister Myrle, as "Mrs. Eldridge," took a sentimental part
She brought tears to our eyes, and touched each human heart.
Naomi Anderson, as prompter, succeeded just fine
She helped them thru so thoroughly that they never missed a line.

May our Home Dramatic Company succeed with the passing years,
And for "All Our Social workers," let's give three hearty cheers!

    (Written in Centerfield, Utah—March 17, about 1926)

Nellie Hunt Collings, about 1929

1926

Amy was just a little past twenty. She was married to Lincoln Avery of Venice, Utah on 23rd Dec 1926. They came up to Centerfield and lived in the old Shoe Shop on the lot next to our house. When Amy's father-in-law, William Avery died, I sent these verses to her mother-in-law:

William Avery

A better, kinder man than he,
It ne'er has been my lot to see.
Strange tho it is, you cannot know,
Why one so good should suffer so.

Each one his burden must bear,
Each one his crown of thorns to wear,
But some complain and fret the while;
Yet he wore his with a smile.

A husband, ever kind and true,
A gentle, loving father too.
His aged mother ne'er could find,
A son who could have been more kind.

A home he built beneath the trees,
Where they might dwell in peace and ease,
They labored hard, did their best,
But each came in at eve to rest.

The very least that can be said,
They'll miss him so, now he is dead.
His task is done, his work is o'er,
On earth he'll toil for them no more.

He's gone ahead, he's on his way,
He could no longer tell death nay,
A home he'll build in some fair dell,
And there in peace with loved ones dwell.

About 1925/26

Here's one I wrote for Ralph and I:

My Dream

I dreamed, sweetheart, that you and I
Were strolling 'neath a summer sky,
We wandered thru a little dell,
A spot we'd both loved very well;

A place we'd known in long ago;
A dell where sweet wild roses grow;
And, O! we were so free from care,
You placed the wild flowers in my hair.

We wandered on, just you and I,
But darker grew the azure sky;
The sky grew black, the air was chill,
The moon had hid behind the hill,

The path was rugged and O! so steep,
 I felt the sharp stones 'neath my feet
And O! how weary I had grown,
I scarce could help but breathe a moan.

It was then, me thought I heard you say,
"Go back, Dear Heart, I've lost the way.
Go back, Dear Heart, go down below,
Back where the sweet wild roses grow."

I shook my head, I answered "No!
Where thou goest I will go,
I gave my heart, my hand to thee,
For life—for all eternity."

You whispered low, I heard you speak,
I felt your warm kiss on my cheek,
"Would I could shield you from all pain,
I've tried, alas, but all in vain.

Go back, Dear One, go down below,
Back where the sweet wild roses grow."
I bowed my head, I murmured, "Nay,
With you, my Dear, I'll ever stay.

"It matters not, whate'er betide,
If only thou art by my side.
Life is not always happiness,
'Tis often more of pain than bliss."

You pressed my hand, methought you spoke,
But, Ah, too soon, I then awoke,
And then, O! how real it all did seem,
I scarce can think—it was a dream!

(Centerfield, Utah)

Ralph and Nellie, 1956

Relief Society Teachers

Yours is a mission of mercy,
Yours is a labor of love,
Yours is a calling, tho humble,
Sent from the Heavens above.

Go to the meek and the aged,
Be thou their staff and rod,
Go to the wayward and erring
Bring them back safe to their God.

As you go forth to your duties
Go with a prayer sincere;
That you may not be found wanting
In the work of the Master Dear.

(Written in Centerfield, Utah)[7]

---

7. RWC notes that "we actually moved to Idaho in the spring of 1927 as we left Centerfield on my 10th birthday—April 12, a day I will never forget." This poem apparently predated the move.

November 1927

We were now living in Jerome County, but we still went into Wendell to church, when we went.

I had a real heartache, when I saw this place for the first time. The first year I was out here I never saw a living soul but my own family from October until March 17th. While the men were working in the Turkey House during the Thanksgiving and Christmas holiday season I composed this tribute to Ralph:

Dear, Old-Fashioned Dad

He is mighty old-fashioned, his notions queer and old;
But, "Let me tell you this, Boys, he has a heart of
   gold."
He don't go in for style, don't follow every fad;
But he's right there,
He's on the square,
That Dear Old-Fashioned Dad.

He's mighty tired and weary and run down at the heel;
But let me tell you this, Boys, you never hear him
   squeal.
He greets you with a smile, Boys, whether things are
   good or bad,
For he's right there,
He's on the square,
That Dear Old-Fashioned Dad.

Things are looking pretty tough just now, for Our Old Man,
So let's put our shoulders to the wheel, and help him all we can.
If we all pull together, Boys, why things won't be so bad.
We'll be right there,
We're on the square
To help out Dear Old Dad.

       (Wendell, Idaho—1927)

Nellie standing outside the
Collings Farmstead in Jerome

About 1930

I wrote several poems while attending Wendell church. As soon as possible after our arrival in the Wendell and Jerome area I learned that my dear friend and benefactor when I was a young girl looking for work, Feen (Josephine) Keeler, was living in Jerome and we renewed our old time friendship. When she had a siege of illness and had to go to the hospital, I wrote these lines for her:

To Mrs. Josephine Keeler

We are praying for you, Dearest, in this, your greatest fight,
And if prayers and faith can save you, you will regain your sight.
The Doctors all seem doubtful, they really cannot tell,
But there's a Greater One who knoweth all things well.

You will never be in darkness, this I truly know,
For the Light within your soul shines with a ruddy glow.
I never yet have told you, just what you are to me,
Perhaps you'll never know, Dear, until Eternity.

Inwards I can't tell you, how my love for you has grown,
But, somehow I have felt, that you I have always known.

I would ask now, Dearest Friend, that you ever be of cheer,
For you have a good kind husband, and children fond and dear.

We have laughed and talked together, down through the coming years.
Though we have often smiled through bitter, scalding tears.
Like ships on Life's great ocean we are drifting with the tide,
When we reach the distant shore, may we then sail side by side.

January 1931

When Ralph's Aunt Augusta Bohman Collings died in Ephraim on 27 January 1931, I had sent these verses to her daughter Sylvia Delight Collings Musig:

To Sylvia

A mother, such as yours, I ween,
Is greater far than any Queen.
While on her bed of pain she lay,
She taught her children day by day,
And with a countenance serene,
She taught of man, of God supreme.

She suffered ill health and pain,
Strength she never more would gain,
But still she prayed that she might live
While advice and aid she yet could give
To her dear children, here below,
And so, it seems, God willed it so.

In every walk, in every clyme,
You hear of Mother Love divine.
But what, to me, seems greater far,
Is the love you children have for her,
The sacrifices you have made
To give your Mother cheer and aid.

Reward to you shall be given,
If not on Earth, Alas, in Heaven,

But, should it not, this I'll say,
Within your hearts you've had your pay.

    (This was written about one of Ralph's aunts who used to live in Monroe, Utah. Written in Jerome, Idaho)

1931

When Jean Jensen, a good friend living in Centerfield, lost her little one, I sent her these verses:

My Child

O! Little Child, God gavest me a gift, gift direct from Heaven art thee.
Of my own flesh and bone thou art, yes! Of my very soul—a part.
A treasure of the rarest gold, He gave to me to carve and mold.
O! Master, great is my task, 'tis almost more than Thou shouldst ask
Of me, I am so meek and frail, I tremble, lest I should fail;
Be near me, Lord, that I may call, O! Help me guide these feet so small.

O! I would ask, My Child, for thee, all that I have yearned to be.
Of wealth, of fame, and success, but, most of all, pure happiness.
My love for you, O! Baby Mine, 'tis a love O! Most Divine.
If natural Mother's love is like this, and fills the soul with purest bliss,
I wonder, as I gaze on thee, how great God's love for all must be.

I dedicate these lines to you, Dearest Jean, so brave and true,
You've a heart of the purest gold, tho in your arms no babe you hold,
You're better, wiser, far, than I, but somehow God has passed you by,
Perhaps He had a task for you, that other Mothers could not do.

February 1933

For her Birthday on the 12th of February 1933, I wrote these greetings to my dear long time friend, Lora Tuft, that I come to know so well, while we were living in Centerfield, but who is now living in our old home down of Monroe:

Birthday Greetings

You're standing today at the top of the hill,
You must ever keep going, you cannot stand still
Tho your way has been rugged and long was the day
You culled the few flowers as you passed on your way.

Where the flowers were faded you gathered the seed;
And cast from your pathway every rank weed.
You thought you would brighten the way as you go,
So things would be easier for those coming below.

But try as you will, that ever will fail
Each one climbing Life's Hill must make his own trail.
A long time ago, you were a tiny girl then,
How happy you were the day you were ten.

You are happy today, much more so, I vow,
For remember, my Dear, you are five times ten, now!
You used to do things that you thought were the style
But now you do things, that are really worth while.

Dreams

I had such wonderful dreams, when I was young and gay.
I knew that I'd be famous in some near future day.
But one bright summer day love came into my life,
First, I was a carefree bride, next, a busy wife.

How the babies crowded in this little house of mine,
Just like so many blossoms clustered on a vine.
With hard and reddened hands I smoothed my aching brow,
And whispered sadly to myself, "Fame—some other day—not now."
Where have they gone, those dreams? They vanished long ago,
Yet, O! I've been so happy, just watching loved ones grow.

About 1933

Ward and Ralph were staying in Wendell at the home of the High School Science Teacher and Athletic Director, Mr. And Mrs. Phil Crutchfield, so they could play football, and be available for practice each evening. The Crutchfields had them do the house work and the dishwashing each day, as both the Crutchfields were teaching. We sent in one of the cows with the boys, along with enough hay to keep her fed for the winter. Her milk, plus a couple of hams and turkeys helped the boys pay for their food bill. [Any extra milk was sold at 10¢ a quart for extra spending money for Ward and me to use—RWC] I wrote the following poem to try and encourage the boys to keep up their efforts at getting an education:

To My Dear Boys

Folks are expectin' a lot from you,
So get in and show 'em what you can do.
Mr. and Mrs. Crutchfield have come to your aid.
Show 'em that you are not afraid
Of work, mental, and physical, too,
Just get in and show 'em just what you can do.

You've got red hair and freckled hide,
But that don't count, if there's brains inside.
Whatever you do, boys, be on the square
Life's a great game, if you'll only play fair.
In the game of life, all cannot win fame.

But to those that love you, don't ever bring shame.

Be clean on the outside, as well as the in,
And tackle each job that you do with a grin.
If things don't turn out, as you wanted it to,
Don't whine that the world is picking on you.
In sailing Life's Ocean, keep a stiff upper lip,
Don't be a drifter, steer your own ship.

The world gives you teachers; books on the shelf;
But for real down right study, get it yourself.
Learn well each lesson, Boys, this you will find,
The half-learned lessons soon slip from your mind.
Do your best, Boys, and whate'er betide,
Mother and Dad will be on your side.
Your loving mother, Nellie Collings

> I have written these lines to you and all other boys who are willing to go to school and face the poverty that you boys are facing. Wendell, Idaho, 1932.

Nellie, Ward, Ralph, and Blanche about 1930
Ralph Willard, about 1935

About 1932

After receiving an editor's rejection slip for some rhyme that I sent in one time, I wrote these words to console myself:

Understood

I thought I'd write a poem once, when I was young, you know.
I sent it to a publisher, a long, long time ago.
There wasn't much to it, a few short tragic rhymes,
I can't remember what was in those simple little lines.

But, as I read it o'er and o'er, I thought it very good,
I hoped that by a few, at least, it might be understood.
The Editor, to my poem, gave neither eye nor ear,
But threw it in a waste basket that was standing near.

And there amid the trash, my wondrous poem lay
Until the stupid janitor came and carried it away.
The janitor was aged, and he was nearly blind,
But he had a heart withall, that was very good and kind.

He read that little piece of mine, and with a gracious smile
Said, "I like your little poem, I love its simple style".
This janitor lived within a hovel poor and small;
But he hung that wretched poem right on his bedroom wall.

I never did receive for it, not one cent of pay;
But my heart was made both sad—and glad by my little poem that day,
I felt that I had found a friend, both wondrous kind and good,
And my little poem and I had both been understood.

March 1933

To honor my Mother's Birthday on 24th of March, 1933, I sent her these lines, which I had written for her while I was down in Centerfield:

To My Mother

It's your birthday today, in that town far away
Your friends are many and true.
I've a family dear in this little town here
But I long to be back home with you.

Tho you live most alone, a Queen on her throne,
Would envy a Mother like mine,
Your children are grown, yet they love that dear home
With its laws and teaching divine.

The friends of my heart, they may ever depart,
Their love may grow cold and chill,
But there is this that I know, that where'er I may go,
That my Mother is loving me still.

I am far, far away from the home town today
And my friends have forgotten me quite;
But dear Mother, I know you're still loving me so,
And you're wondering why I don't write.

O! I know, Mother Dear, that you're waiting to hear
Just some little message from me.
My heart is today, in that home far away,

In that dear little hometown with thee.

I'm a Mother, I own, to children half-grown
And my hair is now streaked with gray,
But my heart ever yearns, and my thoughts ever turn,
To that dear little home far away.

      (Written in Centerfield, Utah)

April 1933

Mother died on 13 April 1933. She was buried on Easter Sunday. I attended her funeral in Monroe. Dallin gave me the money to ride down on the bus. Amy was so glad to see me she cried. For Mother's funeral I wrote these lines:

Our Mother

The day's work is over, eventide has now begun
Tidy up the little cottage, for Mother's work is done.
No more weary feet will tread the kitchen floor
Put away her dear old slippers, she will never need them more.

Her dress and her apron lay them lovingly away,
"Well done, Thou Faithful Servant," can't you hear the Master say?
How many little babies to her bosom she has clasp
The arms that held them tightly, are resting now at last.

She was so tired and weary, we are glad to see her rest.
O! How peacefully she is sleeping, as in snow robes she is dressed.
As children we were happy, free from every thought and care
But as twilight came, Dear Mother, called us home for evening prayer.

When life's day is over, when eventide has just begun
As she calls each name and clearly, may we answer,
  "Here, I come!"

Emily Casto Hunt[8] about 1900

---

8. In the typescript copy of *The Journal of Thomas Hunt* (undated) appears the following tribute:

Emily Casto Hunt

They said she was dead.
That word—no more.
Bewildered and stunned
My thoughts crept home and wandered in
Through my grandmother's parlor door.

Why does one cry at memories
And empty houses with their keepers gone?
Her bed, her peppermints in the dresser drawer,

June 1934

...I forgot to mention that in June of 1934, when Ward was recuperating from his appendicitis operation, he went on a Temple excursion to Salt Lake city, and then went on down to Venice and spent the summer with Amy and Lincoln and family. While he was there with her, the Hunts decided to organize the Thomas Hunt Family by having a Reunion in Monroe, in commemoration of Thomas' 108th birthday. The program, which Amy helped organize was presented on the 16th of June, 1934. I wrote a long story-poem which Ward read as his part in the program:

Her old well-worn rocking chair
Where I was rocked upon her knee
A thousand times or more.
And at her feet I've held her yard
And watched her knit the shawls
For many an unborn great grandchild.

But she was tired and could not stay
To knit the robe for me—my children are too far away.

—Ina Hunt

Our Hunt Grandparents[9]

From England's native shore,
Many long years ago,
Our Grandparents sailed to America
For the Gospel's sake, you know.

The grog-shops and the coal mines,
They left them far behind,
And came to this fair land of ours,
A haven of Peace to find.

When Grandma heard the Gospel
To her it was so grand,
She thought her friends and kinsmen
Would this glorious Truth understand.

But when she tried to tell them
This message pure and bright,
They did not see the grandeur,
To them 'twas far from right.

So, with her husband and babies
She left her native shore.
Her friends and kindred—
She never saw them more.

---

9. This poem also exists in a typescript (undated) of the *Journal of Thomas Hunt*, in which the poem, in the quatrain form reproduced above, appears as an introduction. Following the poem in the typescript is the following: "Written in honor of the one-hundred-eighth birthday anniversary of our pioneer ancestors, Thomas Hunt and his wife Hannah Moon Hunt, and read at the first Thomas Hunt Family Reunion held in Monroe, Utah, 16 June, 1934.

This wild new country
They loved with all their heart;
But from England's ways and customs
They never did depart.

Of their first adventures,
I've never heard them tell,
But after years of bitter struggles,
They came out West to dwell.

Away out here in Utah
They suffered bitter pain,
The grasshoppers and crickets
Robbed them of their grain.

Grandpa became so disheartened,
With so many to be fed,
He humbly to the Bishop
He went, and asked for bread.

The Bishop said, "I'll help you
And do all that's in my power,
But you're a property owner,
We cannot give you flour."

When Grandma heard of this
She was angry, I vow.
"Do thee think, for just one
Sack of flour, I'd sell my only cow?"

On greasewood greens and buttermilk,
The family was fed
And with the butter bought flour
For which to make the bread.

Through all those bitter years,
They both retained their health;
And with their thrift and labor
They gained their share of wealth.

We may not all gain wealth
Nor ever yet gain fame,
But to those Dear Old Kinfolk,
May we never yet bring shame.

That dear Old English name,
Let us keep it from the dirt
That by any fault of ours,
May that dear name ne'er be hurt.

To all you younger children,
It would be easier for you
Could you but know and love them
As we older children do.

While we were still living on the Stephens place, Ralph's cousin, Clarence Bates, son of Nephi James Bates and Sarah Ann Collings, came out to visit us with as much information as he could on the Collings Family. We gave him our family statistics and then I wrote a poem about our Collings ancestors from stories I had gleaned from Ralph's Grandmother, Emma Lawrence Collings, during our many visits while we were living together in Monroe. She often told me of her experiences while coming to "the Land of Promise" and of the hardships she and her family endured in getting here. She died on 7 Dec 1914. Her husband had preceded her in death some 23 years earlier, having died 12 Jul 1891.

Thomas Hunt and Hannah Moon Hunt

Our Collings Grandparents

Many, many years ago, 'neath dear old England's sky,
A man so quiet and serious, and a maiden coy and shy;
Knelt before the Altar there, and became man and wife,
Thus they journeyed on together, thru a long successful life.

What a great undertaking! What a sacrifice to make,
When they left their native land for the dear Gospel's sake.
At last they crossed the ocean, and were safely here on land,
With other Mormon people, they joined the Handcart band.

Far across the wide, wide plains, thru sunshine and storms,
Marched that brave little mother, with a baby in her arms
And the manly little boys trudging at their parent's side;
When they grew tired and weary, their stick horses then would ride.

Long, long days they traveled, with the blue skys over head,
At night oft times they camped with the ground for a bed;
The nights, oft cold and chilly, and bitter grew the blasts,
Oft in the morn, sister Louie's hair to the ground was frozen fast.

With a tiny bit of flour and frozen oxen meat
For days and days together, this was all they had to eat.
After weary days of travel, they felt they were at peace;
But even in fair Utah, their troubles did not cease.

With Indians, crickets, and grasshoppers to fight, they raised their little crew;
But of all that happy family, there's now living only two.
I never knew the father, of him I cannot tell,
But that dear brave little mother, I knew and loved her

well.

She oft sang to my children and taught them English games,
Told stories, 'bout Sam (their Grandpa) whom she'd carried across the plains
Those dear good old Kinfolk have gone to their reward;
May their rest be as peaceful as their labors here were hard.

May all the children's children scattered o'er this bright land,
May they all unite together, and form a happy band.
They gave to you this gospel, with its tidings good and true
Let me say to you, "Grandchildren, there's work for you to do."

Richard and Emma Lawrence Collings

March 1938

The Wendell Ward house was an old lumber building and very much in need of being remodeled. About the first thing we did was to help the rest of the Ward to build it. Just how many years we went to church in it I don't know, but it was a beautiful building and we were very proud of it; but on the Fourth of July 1937 it burned to the ground or might just as well, for all that was left of it was an old black skeliton. We were sure a discouraged Ward, but in due time we built it back up again....

In March 1938, Mrs. Ella Hewlett wrote and asked me if I would write a poem to try and encourage the people, so I wrote the following:

Faith, Our Guiding Star

How many glorious blessings has God on us bestowed
Yet, how oftimes we've murmured at our heavy tiresome load.
If we but remain faithful we shall gain our heart's desire
May our souls be pure and holy, like this building—cleansed with fire!

Let us heed the blessed Gospel, send its messages afar
With God's Prophets, as our teachers and Faith, Our Guiding Star
It will take a lot of courage to win this noble fight
Yet 'twill make our burdens lighter if we keep our star

in sight.

May we attend our meetings as one great happy throng
And give praises to our Father in our prayers, and in our song.
When we meet each Sabbath Morning and our numbers are but few,
Our teachers feel discouraged, and know not what to do.

Let's all work together, let us strive with one accord
To keep our building clean, 'tis the dwelling of the Lord
Launched, but not anchored, in our battles for the right
May we enter in God's harbor with Our Star of Faith in sight.
May Our Star of Faith keep shining, may we see its glimmering ray,
Shining out upon the darkness o'er the hilltops far away.

>(Written on March 17, 1938 for the Wendell Ward, Wendell, Idaho)

Wendell Ward House, about 1936

Wendell Ward, about 1941

August 1941

Aug 2 I went down after the mail this morning, the mail man handed me a telegram telling me that my brother Alvin was dead. He died on the 31st of July. I came home and canned fruit until 5 or 6 o'clock, then got ready and left that evening. I was so tired I just sat and rested for the first 40 or 50 mi. then I even got tired of sitting still. They had his funeral on the 4th. I wrote this poem for the family:

Our Dear Brother

Close his desk, O! gently, Ina, he will never need it more,
Gather up his books and papers, for your Daddy's work is o'er.
Did I say his work was finished, did I say his task was done?
Nay, Lass, I am mistaken, for his work has just begun.

In his office, round the Courthouse, they will miss his familiar face,
But I feel that he's been called, on a more important case.
Yes, they will miss him at the office, yet someone will fill his place,
But at his own fireplace, none can the loneliness efface.

Brothers, Sisters, Friends and Acquaintances, came to him for advice,
So perhaps, some dear one's called from realms of Paradise
To the home where he has gone, has he an office there?
Yes, I think I'll see him twerling in his roomy office chair.

How will he spend his time after his busy office hours?
Angel, can't you spare one corner, where he ma grow his favorite flowers?

July 1942

July 22 It has been a month since I heard from Ralph, it seems so hard, as he has been such a home boy. O! where is my boy tonight?

July 27 Blanche came back from the mail, I wasn't in the house when she came, she called, "Mother," but I knew by her voice that she had a letter from Ralph. I shall always think of this as one of the happiest days of my life.

Ward in the Service, World War II

Ralph in the Service, World War II

* * * * * * *

We haven't any fruit to speak of, but our garden is fairly good, oh there is lots of weeds; we got a good price for the wool and our lambs brought us $600. We are all in the best of health. I forgot to include the following two poems that I have written for the Relief Society:

Why I'm a Member of the Relief Society

Why I'm a member of the Relief Society, perhaps you'd like to know,
And why all its sacred meetings I dearly love them so.
The Relief Society, like our Church, is world wide in its scope
'Tis the key to abundant living and with life's problems, helps up cope.

'Tis an opportunity for self expression, for service, love and truth
The experience of advancing years mingles with the fires of youth.

Sharing ideas with each other helps us to more fully understand
That in the darkest hours of sorrow to give a helping hand.
In this great organization, four courses are outlined
These by lessons in Our Magazine are beautifully defined.
Theology is a challenge to our spiritual and mental lore,
Testimony and knowledge give alike to rich and poor.

Work and Business teaches us to labor and beautify
And the instructions we receive to our homes we can apply.
The chief value of Literature is to broaden and strengthen our life,
And in this world of war and turmoil, gives us relief from toil and strife.
Social Service aids us to so live and make adjustments in our plan
Helps us to dwell in peace with ourselves and with our fellowman.

In sharing the Gospel with others, our Visiting Teachers lead,
Crossing the threshold of homes and giving aid to the

ones in need.

Blue and Gold—Our Banner, may it ever be unfurled!

And the Chorus of Our Singing Mothers, may they echo around the world.

>(Written for Romedel[10] Relief Society Conference—Sept. 1941 or 42)

Let's Keep a Bit of Sunshine Tucked Away Within Our Hearts

Altho' the sun is shining, we cannot see it now
For clouds of sable darkness, are resting on its brow.
With sad and tearful faces we gaze up at the sky
And clasp our hands meekly, and sigh, and sigh, and sigh.
There's nothing we can do to make the clouds depart
So let's keep a bit of sun shine tucked away within our hearts.

The world is filled with hatred, with suffering and war,
But now and then a gleam of hope comes glittering from afar
With eyes filled with anguish, we gaze up at the sky
And clasp our hands in terror, and cry, and cry, and cry.
There's nothing we can do to make the clouds depart
So let's keep a bit of sun shine tucked away within our

---

10. The small branch Nellie was then attending had been formed from members living in Jerome and Wendell...hence the name 'Romedell.'

heart.

A housewife's life is drudgery filled with longing and despair
And when the day's work is over, we sink into our chair.
We see not the brilliant sunset, so radiant in the sky
But bow our heads in weariness, and sigh, and cry, and cry.
But let's rest awhile, and take another start,
And keep a bit of sunshine tucked away within our heart.

(Written in 1942)

About October 1942

Ralph W. Collings

R each out, O! hand of destiny
A nd bring my boy back to me,
L ove they say has a long arm
P ray God, will keep you from all harm
H eaven bring you back to us we pray,

W e'll be watching for you day by day.

C herish and honor, Our Land so free
O! May you ever sing of freedom and liberty
L et peace and happiness reign
L ove, life, and laughter remain
I n this, Fair Land, Let us our praises shout
N ever let our torch burn out
G od Bless you night and day
S oldier Boy for you we pray.

Ralph, in Leyte, Philippines, 1944

About October 1942

Sunshine

I arose bright and early this morning
While the clouds were still bleak and cold
But soon came the glittering sunshine
And turned them into gold.

'Tis ever thus with our hearts
Be they ever so weary and cold
Just a ray of human sunshine
Can brighten them up tenfold.

Why then are we so chary,
In doing a kindly deed?
Why do we often hesitate
To help a friend in need?

Ah! Yes, we will share with the beggar
Our very last slice of bread,
And to the tired traveler
We will oftimes give our bed.

But to our own fellow worker,
As we pass along our way,
Do we ever take the time
A kindly word to say?

To those who are feeble and aged,
Treading slowly down life's long road

Do we ever try to help them;
In lightening their heavy load?

To hearts that are sad and lonely
To souls that are weak and old
Let us be like the glittering sunshine
And turn their dark clouds into gold.

    (I sent this one to Ralph, too)

October 1942

Jerome Ida.
Oct. 15, 1942

Dear Ralph: -

God Bless you, my Soldier Boy
Where ever you may be;
And when the War is over, Dear
May you then come home to me.

> Is, the prayers and wishes
> Of your loving mother,

Nellie Collings

Be of good cheer[11]

---

11. Not from Nellie's diary, this short verse appears in an autograph book sent to Ralph Willard as a Christmas gift in 1942. Other pages include best-wishes from his father, Ralph; Dallin, Bernice, Lelia, and Patsy [Patty] Collings; Blanche and Lin Cooper; William, Leone, Ruth, Leah Ruth, Eugene, Ellen, and Gena Butler; Anna Smith; Leila Weigle; Roland and Vivian King; Lucy and Doris Loy; Freda Roholt; Artie and Emma Barker [Ralph Willard's future uncle- and aunt-in-law]; Esther McFee; and Mrs. J. E. Barker [another future in-law]. Many of these names figure prominently in multiple entries in Nellie's diary.

Oct. 15, 1942.

Dear Ralph: –
God Bless you, my Soldier Boy
Where ever you may be;
And when the War is over, Dear
May you then come home to me.
So, the Prayers and wishes
Of your loving Mother,
Nellie Collings.

(Be of good cheer)

March 1943

Mar 29 Well, things have really been happening lately. Went in to Jerome on the 22nd to Conference, it seemed wonderful to me, I saw so many friends from Wendell and some from Jerome. While I was going in to lunch Sister Williams stopped me and said she had [a] picture of Ralph taken with her son and some other boys, I couldn't eat my dinner, for looking at it. O! yes I wore my pretty new dress I bought with some of the money Ralph gave me. God a fancy new night gown and some stockings (on the 16th). On the 23rd went up to the Butler's to find out where the meeting was going to be held, found out they were coming here, so that meant I would have to clean up my house, as it was really dirty. When we got back, Dad was going in town and wanted me to herd the sheep, I went with him up to Weigle's to borrow a dictionary, so I could write a poem for Ralphie, he wanted me one just for him, I have written one, and am going to write him another:

To My Soldier Boy
[Somewhere in Australia—1943]

A little red box filled with letters
Worth its weight in gold to me,
Love Letters? Yes, Love letters
From My Soldier Boy over the sea.

Most a year now since he left us
And sailed across the sea;

But he's been so good and faithful
Writing letters home to me.

Yesterday I went out looking
For Daddy and the sheep,
And on the COLLINGS[12] Hill
My vigil there to keep.

No green grass was growing
To make the knoll look gay,
Nothing but scraggly sage brush
And rocks all old and gray.

And while I stood there gazing
At each old shabby stone
They had donned green velvet dresses,
With patterns all their own.

And on the ground was strewn,
Sagebrush and willow wood,
I stooped and picked it up,
As only Mother would.[13]

---

12. "Collings Hill" refers to a name constructed of white talc lava rocks by Ralph and Ward in the back fields of the farm near Jerome, Idaho. "When we children were young we collected some of the loose rocks with the white talc on one side and placed them in such a way as to spell the word "COLLINGS" in letters large enough that one could see it from the far end of the field—approximately 300 yards. RWC."

13. Every time Mother went out into the field she always came back with an armful of stovewood or kindling for the fire [RWC not on the holograph copy he received].

A great fluttering in the willows,
But I was frightened then,
When up flew a pheasant,
Perhaps a mother hen.

With the wood that I had gathered,
 I baked a birthday cake,
Not alone for Dad and Me;
But just for Old Time's sake.

Things didn't quite work out
To the old accustomed plan,
For now there was no Laddie
To scrape[14] the cake dough pan

Along Life's rugged pathway,
We, Old Folks have journeyed far
And we'll keep, "Love's Lamp Light" burning
In the cottage, where we are.

We care not for pomp and glory
But this we ever pray,
Our Ralphie will return, as clean a Bonnie Laddie
As the one who went away.

Written for you, and you only
By your loving Mother

---

14. The holograph copy suggests *lick* as an alternate reading; Nellie includes both words in the copy Ralph received

(Written in March; he received it on the 15th of April—3 days after his birthday.)

To my Soldier Boy.
A little red box filled with letters
Worth its weight in gold to me,
Love letters? Yes, love letters
From my Soldier Boy o'er the sea.

Most a year now since he left us
And sailed across the sea;
But he's been so good and faithful
Writing letters home to me.

Yesterday I went out looking
For Daddy and the sheep,
And on the COLLINGS hill
My vigil there to keep.

No green grass was growing
To make the knoll look gay,
Nothing but scraggly sage brush
And rocks all old and gray.

Ralph and Nellie,
with Blanche, Dallin, Ralph Willard,
Berniece, and Lelia
about 1936

About 1943

Our Family

Ralph went to Australia
Ward too sailed on the foam
The rest were scattered here and there
Blanche in a Nurses' Home
Mother stood on the "COLLINGS" hill
Where the grass and wild flowers grow
And felt a loneliness in her heart
That the rest may never know.

> (written while the boys were overseas—possibly in 1943—RWC)

February 1945

Feb 2: ...In one of Ralph's last letters, he wanted me to write a poem for Mrs. Madge Campbell, a young woman in Australia, who was kindness itself to him. And I have just finished it, wish I had some pretty paper and ribbon.

Feb 3: Went in to Jerome, did some shopping, got some fine paper and some red, white and blue ribbon, has a swell time in town, met such a lot of friends, some I visited with, but others I just saw at a distance, but even that means something....

Feb 4: As I was in town all day yesterday I am not even going to let myself get lonesome. This morning have been busy cleaning up the old house. After dinner, sat down and copied the verses, and fixed them up with red, white and blue ribbon. Then wrote a letter to Ralph, and one to my sister Maybell. Went down and mailed Ralph's letter, but didn't have any stamps, went in to see Butler's a min.

Jerome, Idaho
Feb 2, 1945

Sister Madge Campbell
Brisbane, Australia

Dear kind, gracious and unknown friend:
    To you, our heartfelt thanks we send,
For all the kindly things you've done,
    For Ralph, our lonely soldier son.

To a stranger on a distant shore,
    You opened up your cottage door
In your family circle there
    A place for him you did prepare.

From World War cares he then was free
    While your children played about his knee
A sister of the nearest kin
    Could not have been more kind to him.

Let us once more, our thanks impart
    From the very depth of a sincere heart
For bringing both hope and joy
    To the parents of a soldier boy.

Thanks to you, and the Help of God
    He found Our Church on a distant sod
And goodbye, now to you we'll say
    God be with you night and day!

                              Yours very truly

                              Nellie and Ralph Collings[15]

---

15. The above letter-poem was written by Mother to Mr. Allen and Mrs. Madge Campbell, Latter-day Saints, who had befriended Ralph while he was in the service in the Army air Force during World War II and stationed in Brisbane, Australia during the period of July 15, 1942 until October 19, 1944—RWC note

Campbell Family, Brisbane, Australia, 1944

March 1946

For the Scrap-Book

Within the pages of this book
I've placed here where friends may look,
Have chosen with the greatest care
Gems of thought both quaint and rare,
Taken what I thought was best,
And then discarded all the rest.

O! How much better we, if we'd find
A place like this within our mind
Just make of it a garden spot,
A sacred holy little plot,
Where we would plant the best of seeds
And then discard the weeds.

And if God, on The Judgement Day
Would do with us the selfsame way
Life's Book—would kind deeds be written there,
Or would the pages be blank and bare
In writing these lines to you I'd say,
"Do as I say, Not as I do!"

(Written for Lila Neigle on Mar. 14, 1946.)

October 1946

Oct 14: *We Got Our House Electrified Today!*

Put Jackie to sleep, and went down after the mail, told Dad to watch him for me, he was awake when I got back. Dad had him outside where the men were putting in the wires. After dinner Mrs. Thompson came up to see if we were going in town. They were holding their Relief Society as there will be a funeral tomorrow. We went in, but were late, Jackie was as good as gold. When we got home the lights were all turned on. What a beautiful sight!

Collings Farmstead in Jerome ID, about 1942

June 1949

Ralph didn't feel like going to Sunday School, so we stayed home. I killed time the best I could. After dinner wrote letters. Wrote to Ward, Maybell, and Amy. Campbells came up for a while. I wrote a few lines of poetry, which came to my mind today:

The Journey's End

I've come a long way on the road of life
Fulfilling the duties of mother and wife
Life's Highway has not been a flowery bed,
Worked for the living, mourned for the dead.

Ne'er known luxury, ease or wealth,
Blessed with plenty of pluck, and the best of health
A spirit of courage, a heart full of song
Limbs that were sturdy, a back that was strong.

I've climbed most up to the top of the hill
Hoping that loved ones needed me still,
But should they not, Dear Lord, I pray,
I'll never willingly stand in their way.

O! Let me look back on the past with pride
I've blundered a lot; but at least I've tried.
But when I rest, Dear Lord, at the top of the Hill,
May husband, children, and friends be loving me still.

January 1951

Jan 21: It has been blowing all day, washed dishes and mopped my floors, we haven't been out side, only when it was necessary....Haven't seen anyone to talk to. Read to Dad. Listened to the radio.

The wind doth blow,
And we have got snow,
What do the Old Folks
Do then, Poor Things?

They stay out of the Storm
And keep their selves warm
And wait for the spring.

Ralph, Nellie, and a few of their Grandchildren, about 1955

April 1954

A Torch of love

Your soldier boy is home once more
From fighting on a Foreign shore
So peacefully in his grave he lies
He is resting now 'neath friendly skies.

It is good to know that he is here
Our weary lonely hearts to cheer
And now throughout the coming years
We'll strew his grave with flowers and tears.

His labor now on earth is done
God bless, Our Father, Husband, Son
His children will bless their Daddy brave
While placing flowers on his grave.

Let us keep our lives so pure and sweet
That when in Heavenly realms we'll meet
We'll be one happy family there
A home for us he will prepare.

Guide our footsteps day by day
That we may enter the "Way"
That leads us to our Honored Dead
Our own, Our Dearest Darling Fred.

(Written for the Arnoles on April 2, 1954)

January 1956

Jan 10: Today is the day; been working around a little. Amy wanted to go over to Blanche's, so we put our turkey in to roast, while over there had Blanche wave my hair. They talked business then we came home. The turkey hadn't cooked at all, so we warmed some left overs for dinner, had our turkey for supper. Amy's folks and Nelma went to Twin Falls and I took a big long rest. In the afternoon Mrs. Clyde Hanson (Mrs. Arnold) and Freddie came. She gave us a couple of bath towels—yellow ones—beautiful. The kids came while she was here, she couldn't come to our party. Started real early getting ready, I wanted to wait until time to start before we went down, but Dad wanted to go, so we went with the rest. Dad was discouraged and wanted to come home. The man we asked to take charge, didn't get there on time, so I asked Orel Thurson to take charge. (I feel like everyone had a good time). Not a very big crowd, and not too many from Jerome, but some from Twin Falls, Wendell, and a Mr. Will Hutchinson from Buhl. One thing that pleased me was the way Romedell turned out, everyone who could came, or sent a card. Ella Robinson played the piano for Blanche, she also made and trimmed the cake. Had a wonderful program, most of it given by the family; but we had a reading by Thelma Olson, and a song by Adrian Allen. O! thus ends a perfect day! Jewie and Husband came a visited a while with us, she gave us some pillow cases. Carla gave us a purse. The family gave Dad and me a ring.

Jerome, Idaho
Jan 13, 1956

Dear Ward and Dorothy:—

We sent you our picture for a Christmas Gift. Did you get it? We sent one to you and one to Ralph, but as the girls were coming for our Anniversary, we waited until they got here and gave them one. My I hope you got it; if you did write and tell us right away.

Had a wonderful time at our party. Amy, Lincoln, Carla and Burton came on Sunday, we furnished the Program for the Sacrament Meeting. Lincoln gave the opening prayer, Dad bore his testimony, then Carla and Burton sand several songs, Amy gave a big long talk, then Nelma (she came alone on the bus) gave the closing prayer. Then on Tue. We had the following program: Prayer by William Butler...Song...Solo: Carla Sharp...Ralph Collings...Song...Solo: Burton Avery. Poem: Jackie Cooper. Poem: Eileen Cooper. Reading: Thelma Olson, (she or someone wrote the verses about us. Amy has the copies and said she would send it to the rest of you.) Song...Adrian Allen. Duet...Carla Sharp and Burton Avery. 2 songs by Blanche Cooper. She read Matthew's story about Grandma's skating. Then Lin Cooper gave the closing prayer. We all had a good time. My I am sorry you and Ralph and your families couldn't be here. If you can, by all means come down and go to Monroe next summer, we will all go down if we can, if Dad and I are not well enough to go the rest of you can go anyway. We will call it the

Ralph Collings Reunion. I have written so much that my hand is cramping on me. Don't forget to give my love to Dorothy and Matthew and kiss them both for me. My regards to Dorothy's folks. Now be sure and let us know if you received the picture.

Your ever loving Mother
OOOOOO
XXXXXX

Heart's Desire

To a country home in Switzerland the Mormon Elders came,
Bringing with them the Gospel, its wonders to proclaim.
The Book of Mormon stories that these missionaries told
To this eager little maiden were like gems of purest gold,

Among the many missionaries that came to this home to stay
Was our Dear President, Brother David O. McKay.
And still another missionary who came from the new world
Elder Newman won the favor in the eyes of this little Swiss girl!

To the beauties of the Gospel her young heart did aspire
To join the Saints in Utah was now her heart's desire.
When she reached the new land the language she didn't know
But she was brave and courageous, she could work and she could sew.

Again this young man came into her life
And after a few short months of friendship she became his happy wife.
To the sacred altar this maiden was led

And in God's Holy Temple this couple was wed.

In Salt Lake they felt there was no room for them to grow
So with his wife and baby, he came to Idaho.
They reared their little family; one by one their children married
Having family of their own
The Father and Mother were left all alone.[16]

But still they were contented and in peace and comfort did abide
But death came and took him from her side.
This brave little wife and mother, her labors were not o'er
For God called her on a mission to her own dear native shore.

Her work there soon was ended, back to her home she came
Still carrying on the Gospel and teaching just the same.
Here at home she still is working to do her Master's will
Should he call her back again another mission to fulfill.

---

16. Having only a single source for this poem, I am not certain how this anomalous stanza should be treated. It breaks the rhythmical and rhyming patterns in the surrounding stanzas, and as such makes less sense that perhaps it otherwise might.

(I wrote this a while back for Sister Newman, but lost it, but my son found it while looking through a book—1958)[17]

Ralph and Nellie at their Jerome House, about 1960

---

17. Nellie's note.

A Short One

I was invited to a party,
Once upon a time.
They told me I could either
Bake a cake or make a rhyme.

So I decided I had better
Write a verse.
While my poetry is horrid
My cake is worse.

> (This is probably one of the last poems Mother wrote—it was pinned to one of the pages in her anthology of poems—RWC)

June 1960—Final Entries in Nellie's Diary

Jun 7: The milkman came first thing this morning, then Bernice came and took Dad down to shop. Will send Danny's gift with her. Mail-letter from the Telephone. She came back with the groceries, but had to leave and go home.

June 8: Have got my wires crossed, was thinking today was the day, that Bro. Davis and Cunningham were coming to administer to me, but I listened to TV and sure enjoyed it.

June 9: They came—but should have been the Ward Teachers, but they didn't come.

June 10: Bernice's Birthday. I wanted to give her a gift, I thought if Blanche were here I would send one. Grandma is worried because no one came to see me. She said that as much as I have done for the Church, some one should come to see me. Jeanie Weigle lives in the Thrawl place.

June 11: The days have slipped by, and I don't know where they have gone.

June 13: Sandra Deluccia came, taking the names of the Church members. Today is Ward's birthday. I will try and write him a letter. Mrs. Smith and Mrs. Jones called to see me.

APPENDIX I

Ralph Willard's transcription of Nellie's diary concludes with the lines: "Mother and Dad passed away, within a few months of each other, just a few months later."

As an adjunct to the transcription he adds the following transcription of Ralph and Nellie's obituaries and funeral programs:

JEROME, IDAHO—Sept. 7, 1961

Mrs. Nellie Elida Hunt Collings, 78, Jerome, died Wednesday at the Wood River Convalescent Home, Shoshone, after a long illness.

She was born March 4, 1883, in Monroe, Utah and was married to Ralph Collings January 10, 1906, in the Manti, Utah, Temple. They came to Idaho in 1927.[18]

Surviving are her husband; three daughters, Mrs. Lincoln Avery, Venice, Utah; Mrs. Robert Kersey, San Pablo, California and Mrs. Lindell Cooper,

---

18. These two obituaries were typed as they appeared in the local Newspapers and there are some minor discrepancies when comparing one with the other. We actually moved to Idaho in the spring of 1927 as we left Centerfield on my 10th birthday—April 12, a day I would never forget. R. W. Collings

Dietrich; three sons; Dallin R. Collings, Jerome, Ward L. Collings, Perrysburg, Ohio; Ralph W. Collings, Carmichael, California; two sisters; Mrs. Maybel Torgenson and Mrs. Myrle Payne, both Monroe, Utah; 22 grandchildren and 26 great grandchildren.

Funeral services will be held at 11 a.m. Saturday at the Jerome, L.D.S. Second Ward Chapel with Bishop Herrick Drake officiating. Final rites will be held in the Shoshone cemetery. Friends may call at the Wiley Funeral Chapel, Jerome from 1 p.m. Friday until time of Services.

SHOSHONE, IDAHO—Jan. 11, 1962

Ralph Collings, 82, died early Thursday morning at the McWillis Nursing home here. He had been a patient in the home since Sept. 19.

Surviving are three sons: Dallin Collings, Jerome; Ward Lawrence Collings, Rossford, Ohio and Ralph W. Collings, Carmichael, California; three daughters, Mrs. Amy Avery, Venice, Utah; Mrs. Nelma Kersey, San Pablo, California and Mrs. Lindell Cooper, Dietrich, Idaho; 22 grandchildren and 29 great grandchildren.

Funeral services will be conducted at 10 a.m. Tuesday in the Shoshone L.D.S. Church by Bishop Walter Bowman, Dietrich. Concluding rites will be held at the Shoshone Cemetery. Friends may call at McGoldrick Funeral Home Monday evening and until time of services Tuesday.

Mr. Collings was born August 26, 1879, at Monroe,

Utah. He had resided at Jerome, since 1926. His wife, Mrs. Nellie Hunt Collings, died in September 1961.

Funeral Services:
In Memory of
Nellie Elida Hunt Collings

Born: March 4, 1883
Passed Away: Sept. 6, 1961

Services: Sept. 9, 1961—11:00 A.M.

From: Jerome L.D.S. Second Ward Chapel
Officiating: Bishop Herrick M. Drake

Casket Bearers:
    J. R. Pettit
    Earl E. Davis
    Calvin Neal
    J. Cliff Thompson
    Willis Thompson
    Forrest Dixon

Final Rites in the Shoshone Cemetery.

****

Vocal Solo: "That Wonderful Mother of Mine," sung
   by Melba Jackson
Invocation: Leo Olson
Obituary: Thelma Olson
Speaker: William Butler
Song: "Abide With Me"

Sung by: Wayne Thompson
Cliff Thompson
Raymond Jones
Frank Walker

Organist: Thora Gough
Benediction: John Buttars
Grave Dedication: H. Thomas Newman

Funeral Services: In Memory of Ralph Collings

Born: Aug. 26, 1879
Passed away: Jan. 11, 1962

Services: Jan. 16, 1962—10:00 A.M.

From: Shoshone L. D. S. Church
Under direction of Dietrich Ward,
Pres. Glen Sorenson conducting

Pall Bearers:
    J. R. Pettit
    Joe Springer
    Calvin Neal
    J. Cliff Thompson
    Willis Thompson
    Forrest Dixon

****

Solo: "Jesus, Lover of My Soul," sung by Patricia Paulson
Invocation: Gail P. Hendrickson
Obituary: William B. Butler
Speaker: H. Thomas Newman
Duet: "Abide With Me"
    Sung by Nancy and Donna Roice
    Accompanied by Velma Allen

Benediction: A. Leo Olson
Dedication of the Grave: Deral Haycock

Prelude and Postlude: Mrs. Ruth Dillie
Flowers Arranged by: Dietrich M. I. A.
Memorial Book Attendant: Muriel Reynolds
Interment: Shoshone Cemetery
Funeral Directors: Francis M. Bergin

APPENDIX II

Patriarchal Blessing Given to Ralph Collings in Monroe, Sevier County, Utah, March 22, 1903

A Blessing given by Patriarch Robt. F. Goold

Upon the head of Ralph Collins [Collings], son of Samuel Willard and Elizabeth Bertlesen Collins [Collings]. Born August 26, 1879, Monroe, Sevier Co., Utah

Bro. Collins [Collings], in accordance with your request, and agreeable to the Patriarchal Priesthood here established on the earth, in the Church of Jesus Christ, I now place my hands upon your head and give unto you a Patriarchal Blessing. It is well pleasing unto the Lord that you have in the days of your youth, and early manhood, that you have at this time sought to know his mind and will concerning your future life upon the earth. I say unto you that you are of Ephraim, a lawful heir to the Holy Priesthood, privileges and blessings of the Gospel. You have been selected of the Lord to become a power in Israel to proclaim his

Gospel to the Children of Men; It will be the joy and delight of your life, to lift your voice long and loud in the defense of the principles of the Everlasting Gospel. And I say unto you there are great possibilities in the future of life to become an honored instrument in the hands of the Lord to assist in establishing a reign of truth and righteousness upon the Earth, And to this end he has endowed you with rare powers of mind, quick in perception and comprehension, they have been committed to you as a rare gift. And the Lord will hold you responsible for the use you make of them. Therefore, I say unto you, use all due diligence to cultivate the same, that you may have power through the inspiration of the Holy Ghost, to go forth in the strength of Israel's God, to fill with honor the mission you have been called to perform, and which in due time you will be called to by the holy priesthood. Dear Brother, draw near unto the Lord in sacred and fervent prayer, and you shall be clothed with power, that will be marvelous in your own eyes. Your days will be many on Earth, and your life will be shielded from the ravages of disease that are now abroad upon the face of the earth. And I say unto you the Spirit of the Lord shall be with you to such a degree that you will become fearless in the advocacy of the Everlasting Gospel. You will be warned through the inspiration of the Holy Ghost of approaching dangers in your labors in the ministry so that you may be able to detect every evil influence and spirit that may seek to arrest your progress associated with the work of God, and I say unto you dear brother that you must shun all evil associations as you would the presence of a serpent. Your life must be one of purity before the Lord, so that you may be able successfully to perform all that the Lord has designed you should accomplish. And I say unto you dear brother seek unto the Lord for that great and glorious gift of the Gospel, Wisdom, to govern all your conversations and acts in life. And it shall be given you in rich abundance, you shall be successful in all labors in the Ministry, and bring many souls to a knowledge of the truth, and through your faithfulness you will have a part in the First Resurrection and live and reign with the Great Redeemer through the Millennium.

I now seal upon your head every blessing that have been pronounced upon your head at this time on condition of your faithfulness in keeping the Commandments of God, In the name of Jesus Christ, Amen.

APPENDIX III

The final entry in Ralph Willard's typescript was a tribute to Nellie in the form of a poem. The poem was anonymous, but Ralph suggests that it was probably written by Leone Butler.

This final meeting of the summer
    The new one in our Hall of Fame
Came from Monroe, in Southern Utah
    And Nellie Collings is her name.

One of those rare and luck people
    You sometimes meet along the way
Whose husband brings her to meeting
    Long past their Golden Wedding Day.

And Sister Collings, who had always
    Loved to read, and wrote a bit,
Would give the Literary lessons
    In a special way that made a hit.

She helped with quilting, went block teaching
    And saw that her kids were clean and dressed
To go to Sunday School and Mutual

In Barker's Basement, with the rest.

One Sunday they remember
    With Brother Mason up to preach
And one whole bench filled with visitors
    Whose every move made the boards screech.

Did Brother Mason stop his preaching?
    Why no, he scarcely stopped to frown,
But calmly quoted from the Scriptures
    "And the walls came tumbling down."

Depression years were finally over
    And folks could buy a car and gas
The Romedell Branch had filled its purpose
    It's now a memory of the past.

That little loving Branch of Romedell
    Has left a mark on many lives,
The things they learned in that old basement
    Made better parents, husbands, wives.

Now Collingses are both retired
    The farm work they can do no more
But on Relief Society Thursdays
    He still comes chugging in the car.

And brings his Nellie to the Meetings
    And waits around to take her home.
Right now he is in the shade by Tilby's
    So we had better end this poem.

INDEX OF NAMES AND POEMS

[Titles of Poems are given in SMALL CAPS]

Avery, William, 56
Bates, Clarence, 86
Bates, Nephi James, 86
Bates, Sarah Ann Collings, 86
BIRTHDAY GREETINGS, 71
Campbell, Madge, 113
Casto, Emily, 18
Collings Hill, 108n
Collings, Amy, 19, 49
Collings, Augusta Bohman, 67
Collings, Berniece Smith, 111
Collings, Blanche, 75, 111
Collings, Burton Hunt, 41
Collings, Dallin, 80, 111
Collings, Emma Lawrence, 86, 90
Collings, Lelia, 111
Collings, Nellie Hunt, 18, 20, 32, 55, 60, 64, 75, 111, 120, 125, 128; Obituary, 131; Funeral Service, 134; Headstone, 138

Collings, Ralph, 25, 32, 60, 62, 75, 111, 120; Obituary, 132; Headstone, 138; Blessing, 139
Collings, Ralph Willard, 75, 97, 102, 105, 107, 125, 128
Collings, Richard, 90
Collings, Ward, 75, 82, 96, 123
DEAR KIND, GRACIOUS AND UNKNOWN FRIEND, 113
DEAR, OLD-FASHIONED DAD, 62
DREAMS, 72
EMILY CASTO HUNT, 81n
FAITH, OUR GUIDING STAR, 91
FINAL MEETING OF THE SUMMER, THE, 143
FOR THE SCRAP-BOOK, 116
HAPPINESS: A RECIPE, 24
HEART'S DESIRE, 125
HEARTS BEREFT, 46
Hewlett, Ella, 91
HOME DRAMATIC COMPANY, THE, 53
Hunt, Alvin, 20, 94
Hunt, Ed, 20
Hunt, Emily Casto, 81
Hunt, George, 20, 28-29
Hunt, Hannah Moon, 83n
Hunt, Howard, 20
Hunt, Moroni, 18
Hunt, Thomas, 82, 83n
Jensen, Jean, 69
Jones, Delile, 39
Jones, Vern, 39
JOURNEY'S END, THE, 118
Keeler, Josephine, 65

LaRocke, Gwendolyn, 26
Let's Keep a Bit of Sunshine Tucked Away Within Our Hearts, 99
Little Virginia, 47
Missionary Poem, A, 28
Mountain Rose, 35
Musig, Sylvia Delight Collings, 67
My Child, 69
My Dream, 58
My Lost Love, 49
Naser, Ed, 36
Neigle, Lila, 116
Newby, Zelda, 26
Olson, A. Leo, 48
On First Seeing Photographs of My Grandfather..., 15
Our Annual Day, 52
Our Collings Grandparents, 87
Our Dear Brother, 94
Our Family, 112
Our Hunt Grandparents, 83
Our Little Bird, 37
Our Mother, 80
Pettit, Joyce, 48
Prayer, A, 40
Ralph W. Collings, 101
Ransom, Thomas, 37
Relief Society Teachers, 61
Short One, A, 129
Spanish-American War, 19

Sunbeam, 26
Sunshine, 103
That Dear Little Boy of Mine, 41
To Mrs. Josephine Keeler, 62
To My Dear Boys, 73
To My Dear Husband, 31
To My Mother, 78
To My Soldier Boy, 107
To Nellie—from the Perspective of a Century, 13
To Sylvia, 67
Token of Love, A—"Within the Master's Garden...," 44
Token of Love, A—For Nonie, 39
Torch of Love, A, 121
Tuft, Lora, 48, 71
Two Flowers, 21
Understood, 76
Warnock, Maggie, 18
Why I'm a Member of the Relief Society, 97
William Avery, 56
Wind Doth Blow, The, 119

www.ingramcontent.com/pod-product-compliance
Lightning Source LLC
LaVergne TN
LVHW041627070426
835507LV00008B/486